An artist's year in the Harris Garden

Jenny Halstead studied Art and Design at the Sutton & Cheam School of Art followed by a Guest Scholarship at the Royal Academy Schools, London. She then trained and worked as a medical artist and natural history illustrator, but for the last decade has enjoyed the freedom of expressing herself across a much wider spectrum.

She is well-known and widely admired, nationally and internationally, for her draughtsmanship, her modelling of detail and her use of colour. She is a Fellow of the Medical Artists' Association of GB and a Member of the Pastel Society UK.

GW00777133

An artist's year in the
Harris Garden

Jenny Halstead

TWO
RIVERS
PRESS

First published in the UK in 2013 by

Two Rivers Press
7 Denmark Road
Reading RG1 5PA
www.tworiverspress.com

ISBN 978-1-901677-87-4

1 2 3 4 5 6 7 8 9

Two Rivers Press is represented in the UK by Inpress Ltd
and distributed by Central Books.

Cover illustration by Jenny Halstead
Text and cover design by Nadja Guggi and typeset in Pollen

Printed and bound in Great Britain by Ashford Colour Press, Gosport

To be an Artist in Residence in a beautiful garden for a whole year is an honour and a pleasure. A garden needs a witness to bring it to life, and Jenny is a very good one who has done just that, using her vision to represent the seasonal changes, and to depict the people who work in the garden, highlighting things not immediately apparent. She and the staff are a team proud to work together. Her images cover a splendid range of subjects, and are not just vivid, but exciting.

Anthony Eyton RA

Acknowledgements

Firstly I should like to thank the Friends of the Harris Garden for supporting my idea of being Artist in Residence and for sponsoring the publication of this book. I am very grateful to Trevor Pitman, Chairman of the Friends, for his enthusiastic response to the project; to Ann Derbyshire for her help and friendship; and to Giles Reynolds, Pete Tipping and all the volunteers for making me welcome.

Parallel with the launch of this book there is an exhibition at the Museum of English Rural Life (May – June 2013). My thanks to all the staff there and I am very grateful for the financial support of the University Arts Committee.

Special thanks to Richard Bisgrove, Adrian Blamires, and Anthony Eyton for contributing so willingly and so memorably to this book, and to Ann Westgarth for all her help at every point along the way. Credit too to the wonderful team at Two Rivers Press, particularly Sally Mortimore, Nadja Guggi, and Barbara Morris.

My son Tom has been a great encouragement and help; so too my friend Rita. And my partner John has believed in me throughout, and has of course cast his judicious eye over everything. Thank you.

An artist in the Harris Garden

There is a special, almost secret, garden at the far corner of the Whiteknights campus. I cherish my early Sunday morning visits, offering peace and solitude, a pleasure at any time of the year but in high summer the meadow is breathtaking in its beauty. I have the Garden to myself ... it's mine!

This Garden is a *composed* space; it has formal borders with curving hedges that open out on to the wildness of the Prairie Garden, and beyond, the meadows. Woodlands of rare trees, water in pond and stream, a 'jungle' garden, a walled garden.

Paradise is often depicted as a garden, and I see it as a metaphor for self and soul. A safe haven, yet one is encouraged to go on a journey, to feel the excitement of being lost, and entering into another world. But all the time safe within its boundaries.

In Pursuit of Spring.
Oil, 30 × 30 cm

Left: *Pen & watercolour sketch*
Right: **Towards the Wildness**.
Prairie Garden of flowering
Rudbeckia, which opens onto the
Meadow. *Pastel, 32 × 32 cm*

As Degas once said, 'even in front of nature, one must compose'. This means that even in a single sketch, one is already making decisions on what to include. I want this project to be a response to the Garden, *not* research, so I like to work fast with a sketchbook and pen and wash or watercolour, which give me all I need to take sketches through to a finished painting if I so choose. To draw one must observe; it is an intense exercise, the eyes and the brain filtering information, light, shadows, form, structure ... and the hand moving to record the data. Once drawn, it is stamped on one's memory forever. I can look at old sketch books and open them at random ... I am back there, remembering the place, the feel, the sounds, the moment.

I have endeavoured to recreate in my choice of subject matter the mood of the Garden, as affected naturally by seasons and by the weather. The cool shades of winter giving way to the acid fresh greens of spring, followed by the intense radiance and splendour of summer, and finally the orange, browns and parched creams of autumn and back to frosty cold and the cycle is reborn. Where to start? Where to end?

My project

The idea of this project – *'an Artist in Residence'* – came about principally because I liked the idea of observing a garden throughout a year. No, I have not lived in a tent under the trees! The Harris Garden, though still not widely known, has come into its own since 2010 after being redesigned and reworked with new plantings. It has a dedicated Head Gardener, Pete Tipping, working under the expert guidance of Giles Reynolds, Head of University Grounds. Alongside them works an enthusiastic team of volunteers. A tranquil place, but with much hidden excitement, which I hope I have captured.

The year-long project brought together my skills as, initially, a medical artist and natural history illustrator, subsequently enjoying the freedom of being a painter in oils and pastels. I did not wish to represent the Garden in botanical studies but rather as my own interpretation, over the seasons, of this unique twelve-acre space set within the campus of an urban university.

I started at Sutton and Cheam School of Art (which produced two Royal Academicians). Three years, covering a wide variety of skills, and it was at the end of this course that I knew my first love was drawing and the figure or human form in particular, and that I wanted to take this into a profession which offered something useful in terms of illustration. It took time to find out how the illustrations in medical and anatomy books were done and who did them! Longer to find out how one might train.

At the same time I won a Guest Scholarship at the RA Schools and was offered the freedom of the Drawing Schools by the Keeper at the time, Sir Henry Rushbury.

I eventually found Mary Barber, who originally had graduated from the RA Schools just prior to the Second World War, and who was immediately recruited as a Land Girl for a year or so before she was reclaimed by doctors and surgeons to start recording (for teaching purposes) new techniques, facial reconstructions

Pete. Pete outside his shed writing up garden notes. *Conte*, 32 × 40 cm

and basic illustrations for the training of many more doctors, surgeons and nurses. So it was with her, many years later at the Central Middlesex Hospital, that I served my 'apprenticeship', learning to observe and to record operative procedures, drawing fast but accurately. As a medical artist one cannot draw what one does not understand, so a drawing can bring together many elements: one can select, simplify or add relevant anatomy to explain a three-hour procedure in a single drawing, something a photograph could not do as it records the scene as it is.

I worked in various London teaching hospitals illustrating for surgeons, anatomists and physicians and as a one-man band, doing exhibitions and designs for publications. Then, marrying a palaeontologist offered me the opportunity of looking at and drawing rocks and fossils and studying those wonderful things ... dinosaurs. Once again accuracy was required. I decided to turn freelance, working on three editions of *Gray's Anatomy*, and with my husband on various publications including a series of dinosaur books for children.

We were among the first individuals invited to Peking (now Beijing) after the Cultural Revolution. The discussion was over a very primitive fossil fish, and East and West had different ideas on interpretation. The Chinese palaeontologist allowed me to draw this recently discovered beautiful specimen, a naturally formed replica in iron of the blood vessels, nerves, brain and inner ear of a Galeaspid, which had lived some 400 million years ago. The Chinese scientists believed that because I had an understanding of anatomy, this meant I could see the structure of the fossil clearly and was unbiased. It was because of this that the two sides came to an agreement, and it led to the first Anglo-Chinese collaborative paper, which was published in *Nature* in 1979.

The Millennium seat
awaiting visitors. *Watercolour*

The year 2000 and a new millennium: publishing was already digital and moving on fast and I did not wish to work on screen. I felt this was the catalyst I needed to go back to painting. I wanted to use colour in any way I chose. So I took the plunge. I was ready to move from discipline to freedom.

Thus began a new journey.

A walk – more than meets the eye

The gates of the Harris Garden require you to stop, and yet they welcome you to enter and to view what is beyond. The path leads you along and the space opens up to lawns and a vista of trees, magnolia and eucalyptus, and in early spring the brilliance of yellow witch hazel and broom, the new Fragrant Garden and the sound of bird song.

The crab apple orchard (*Malus sylvestris*) is now to our left, having a ground display of spring bulbs then summer grasses, and in a far corner the stunning blue/purple of the brief-flowering hyacinth tree. Now the path divides. Straight on to the pond? Or right, up past the wide herbaceous border to Pete's shed, passing the giant eucalyptus and the newly planted Gravel Garden. Left now to the Formal Garden, passing the Red Border and into the symmetry of the White Garden with Jon Roberts's wooden sculpture '*Meteor*' at its centre, which always reminds me of the skull of *Triceratops*.

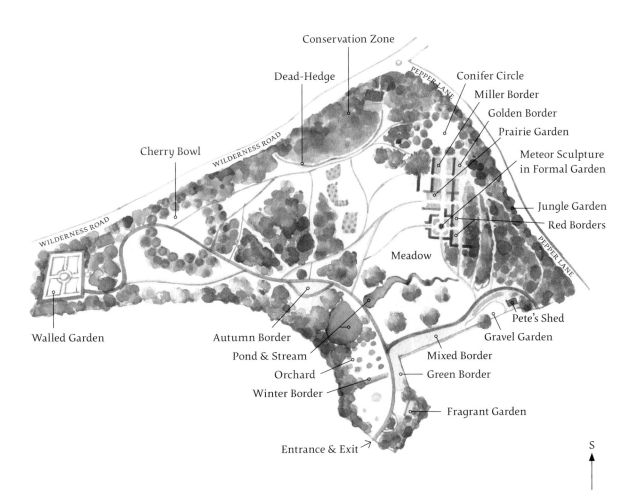

Conservation Zone

Dead-Hedge

PEPPER LANE

Conifer Circle

Miller Border

Golden Border

Prairie Garden

Meteor Sculpture
in Formal Garden

Cherry Bowl

WILDERNESS ROAD

Jungle Garden

Red Borders

WILDERNESS ROAD

PEPPER LANE

Meadow

Pete's Shed

Walled Garden

Autumn Border

Pond & Stream

Orchard

Winter Border

Gravel Garden

Mixed Border

Green Border

Fragrant Garden

Entrance & Exit

S

Opposite page

Left: Towards the Harris Garden.

Watercolour

Meteor sculpture

Right: **Between the Stream and the
Pond.** Weeks of rain. *Pastel*, 32 × 32 cm

Left: Conservation Zone enclosed by the Dead-Hedge. *Pen & wash*
Right: Part of the circle of conifers. *Pen & wash*

Strong-shaped formal hedges of yew and beech protect borders alive with colour in the summer months, or dried brown, catching winter sun through their fronds. The circle of conifers, all different varieties, before us like an audience awaiting a performance!

Turn left across one of the mown grass paths through the splendour of the meadow, in spring filled with bulbs, in summer grasses and flowers. Then woodland, and at the perimeter of the Garden, the Conservation Zone. Now to the majestic cherry circle (known as the Cherry Bowl) and towards more woodland and finally the Walled Garden (open only on Open Days).

Left: Visitors in the shade of the turkey oak with its swinging bough – a child's delight. *Watercolour*
Right: Inside the Walled Garden. *Watercolour*

Back on a grass path through the cherries, past two trees with attractive red bark known commonly as the hybrid strawberry tree, a curved woodchip path leads us through the Autumn Border, back on to the compacted path leading to the pond and the stream under the Caucasian alder and the turkey oaks. And then back to the real world again ...

Winter

The frost receives my print, records a trail
Between stark borders – spike and husk and rag,
Rustle and rattle of seedpod and deadhead –
Past a row of yellow hoses tightly wound,
Wheelbarrows, noses to the ground,
Along a stream of oakleaf, dry and pale,
To where grey suffering Gunneras sag,
Elephantine, over a pond of lead.

One January, in snow, the Walled Garden
Was pared, stalk, stubble, to the quick,
No sign of life until a single jay's
Hop and splay – steely propitious guardian –
And that tiny toadflax drew my gaze,
Head-high: home a mossgrown frostblown brick.

Adrian Blamires

A Touch of Frost. The Garden
entrance – might the sun break
through later? *Oil*, 50 × 50 cm

Shed at Sunset.
Reflected light
from the late
afternoon snowfall.
Pastel, 20 × 28 cm

Below left: Poly-tunnel used in winter. *Pen & wash*
Below right: Crab apples and snowdrops. *Watercolour*

January

A quiet month, the start of my year.

A hard frost today giving a petrified look to the Garden as I enter, everything motionless. A glimmer of sunshine through a chill mist. The sketching has to be fast as my fingers numb. But on a warmer day I would be greeted at the entrance by the sweet and surprising perfume of the *Sarcococca*.

In dull dark January it's always exciting to see a ground cover of snowdrops, small and seemingly so delicate, yet able to thrive in frost and snow and here, above them, like jewels, sizzling red crab apples still on the trees.

Starkness – most trees without foliage, borders without bloom, trimmed neatly down to ground level ready for new growth. The meadow without content. And yet in the formal borders the tall dried grasses stand covered by frost.

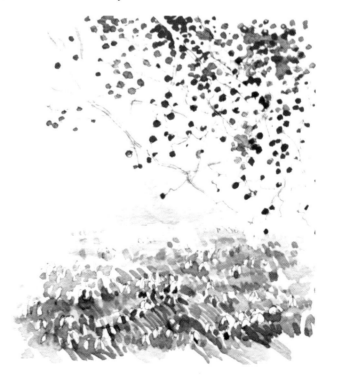

Below left: Winter protection.
Watercolour
Below right: **Snow in the Jungle**.
Pastel, 20 × 28 cm

February

I am always thrilled by snow, not by the discomfort it causes but because it does visually transform the landscape; and it fell, by Saturday afternoon, as predicted. I couldn't wait to get out into the Garden and catch the late afternoon light, a warm glow reflected off the snow through the dormant clematis plants, the snow now levelling the reconstructed area of the Gravel Garden. Sunday morning I was in the Jungle Garden, excited to see the beautiful shapes of the 'tropical' foliage defined now by this covering of white, and I enjoyed making the first steps into it. Yuccas and eucalyptus, palms and fig, gingers and bamboo, frozen, in contrast to the bananas lovingly wrapped in their winter covers. Over to the other side of the Garden the vivid colours of the dogwoods.

Two weeks of freezing temperatures. And only then was it possible to plant wild flower plugs in the meadow and three small oak trees.

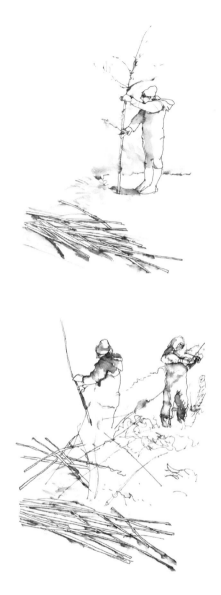

Right: **Dogwoods**. Snow sitting heavily on branches. *Pastel,* 20 × 28 cm

Above: Early spring bulbs
Right: **Shadowlines**. Early signs of spring. *Oil, 30 × 30 cm*

Opposite page
In Leaf and Flower. Daffodils in bloom in the meadow and others still to flower. *Oil, 30 × 30 cm*

March

The snow and frost gone and warmer dry conditions arrive: a real spring-time thrill to enter the meadow, swathed now with white daffodils. A low spring sun shining on the first magnolias and early rhododendrons, with just an indication of leaf on the birches. The 'species' tulips planted in November looking like colourful toys strewn over the far meadow – there were 50,000 bulbs planted in the main meadow in 2010 and more in 2011, they tell me – and the cherry trees at last beginning to show signs of blossom.

The Conservation Zone, also known as the Eco-Zone, has now been defined by a 'dead-hedge', creating a conservation area and a habitat for wildlife. It is quite ingenious and very beautiful; two rows of stakes have been driven into the ground and the centre has been filled by stacking all the dead wood, cut and fallen timber. The area will be planted with hazel later in the year.

The pond bursting into life, foliage appearing in the water and on the banks, coots and mallards foraging and nesting. That iridescent light through new growth and leaf and the tall grasses I particularly love, cleared from the border ready for regrowth.

The Gravel Garden through the year

It has been great to watch the transformation of this space from an overgrown area of tangled shrubs, hops and brambles through to a finished garden. The process entailed initially moving any usable plants, cutting to ground level by hand and then with the aid of a small digger removing roots and turning the ground, which was left to overwinter. By early spring it was levelled, the fence was repaired, and a new beech hedge was planted all along the west boundary as a backdrop for the long Mixed Border and the Gravel Garden. Four trees were planted.

In April the ground and the paths were marked out, and the beds dressed and rotated with sharp sand for soil drainage. By early May it was being planted up, to be followed by a layer of shingle. Plants love this wet warm weather and by June this garden looked well developed and really beautiful, flanked as it was by the beds of peonies, clematis and dog roses. And with the Millennium seat inviting visitors to sit and enjoy.

Opposite page
Above: Digger at work.
Watercolour
Below left: New fence.
Watercolour
Below right: The new
design. *Watercolour*

Right: **Clearing**.
The area to become
the Gravel Garden.
Pastel, 23 × 28 cm

Spring

Japanese woodblock: white blossom on blue,
An upside-down bullfinch's haiku-song.
April at last. Hand in hand, we stroll
A new-mown path round the Cherry Bowl,
Leaving our son to run ahead, run
Full circle, until, shoes soaked in dew,
He zooms up, zaps by, and the race is on,
One I think I can win – but not for long.

Last year, the Garden's Great White Cherry,
Blossom-heavy, -heady, lost a bough
One night of storm, crushing (softly) the very
Bench we'd picnicked on the day before.
Such annihilating abundance! We vow
To make of each succeeding year the more.

Adrian Blamires

Visitors. The meadow path
through the blue *Echium
vulgaris. Pastel,* 32 × 32 cm

April

After months of unusually dry conditions, the hosepipe ban came into force in the first week for most of us (but not for the Garden). Immediately after: the heavens opened and the rain hardly stopped for two months!

There are Open Days once a month, on the second Sunday in the month, starting in early April through to September. The money raised is for various charities.

The first Open Day was reasonably fine and a large number of visitors availed themselves of all the super plants for sale ... which your garden just could not live without!

Walking towards the Cherry Bowl, I saw before me the magical white blossom almost solid in its density and yet still so delicate; the other trees still without leaf throwing narrow shadows across the ground.

Right: **Blossom in the Cherry Bowl**.
Oil, 50 × 50 cm
Below: Sketch for finished painting.
Watercolour

Above left: Harris Garden Open Day and Plant Sale. *Pen & wash*
Above right: **Plant Sale**. Visitors selecting plants at one of the six Open Days. *Pastel*, 23 × 23 cm
Below: Banana plant. *Watercolour*

The University organised their own Open Day in the Harris Garden at the end of this month, where (as Artist in Residence) I was asked to show sketches and some completed work, in a gazebo (with additional polythene flaps specially added for protection!). This event also planned to have music, entertainment, teas and an ice cream stall, as well as offering advice on planting and making bee 'hotels' (a tied bundle of canes, hung in a tree, offering a resting place for bees and insects). But sadly it was cancelled due to high winds following torrential rain, causing the turkey oaks to dramatically shed their branches.

And yet the Garden thrived in the rain, the spring flowers continued blooming, daffodils in the meadows, early bluebells in the woodlands and the crab-apple trees in blossom in the orchard.

The frost protection was removed from the bananas ... Might summer be on its way?

Flowering highlights:
· Indian mallow (*Abutilon x suntense*)
· Alliums
· Candelabra primulas
· Paper handkerchief tree (*Davidia involucrata*)
· Geraniums
· Avens (*Geum*)
· Blood grass (*Imperata cylindrica* 'Rubra')
· Iris
· Pheasant's eye narcissus (*Narcissus poeticus* var. *recurvus*)
· Mixed Border
· Meadows
· Stream

May

A delicious month of growth and fresh colours, the smell of cut grass and trimmed hedges and the sound of birdsong.

After a week or so away, the contrast is stunning, the meadow grasses have grown, intertwined with early meadow flowers. Tall elegant yellow irises by the stream, the Mixed Border bursting into flower and the amazing paper handkerchief tree by the formal hedges now in full splendour.

The beautiful colour combination of dark green hedges guarding the stately white lupins, under-planted with silver grey grasses in the White Garden, is an unexpected delight, inspirational in its simplicity.

An added attraction in late May was the barbecue laid on as a thank-you to the volunteers, with three large barbecues cooking some delicious spicy food. With salad and strawberries, it made a perfect end to that morning's labours.

Opposite page
Below left: A barbeque to thank
the volunteers. *Pen & wash*
Below right: **Reading**. The first
flowering of the Gravel Garden.
Pastel, 32 × 32 cm

Above & right: The Gravel Garden
in bloom. *Watercolour and Pen
& watercolour*

Flowering highlights:
· Golden marguerite (*Anthemis tinctoria* 'E. C. Buxton')
· Camassias
· Candelabra primulas
· Tree anemone (*Carpenteria californica*)
· Foxgloves
· Hostas
· Roses
· Wild flower meadows
· Mixed Border
· Stream

Below: Three views of the stream in winter, early spring and summer. *Watercolour*

Opposite page
Above left: Digitalis. Watercolour
Above right: Gunnera. Watercolour
Below left: **Time of the Lilies**.
Oil, 30 × 30 cm
Below right: The sound of summer. *Watercolour*

June

A magnificent bank of wild foxgloves greets me as I enter – purples, pinks and whites which sway haughtily in the breeze, fringed by the cool blue geraniums. A contrast to the odd self-sown ones in my own garden, which appear (and are still most welcome) in all the wrong places! Walking along the mowed grass paths towards the meadow, an amazing sight, a sea of blue mist (*Echium vulgaris*) popularly known as Viper's Bugloss, mixed with white daisies, grasses and butterflies.

The stream at last has come into its own, since it was cleared and regravelled in winter, with its banks built up to accommodate bulbs, now transformed by magnificent yellow irises to give it height and structure.

Beds filled with plants of so many varieties, with colours changing as one dies back and another takes over. There could be a subject to paint on any and every day!

Garden bee

Honey bee

The pond through the year

Sitting now by the pond, enjoying the magnificent *Gunnera* (giant rhubarb), with the sun shining through its massive leaves, it's hard to remember it in winter and that it will shortly die back as if wounded, and fall to earth, stalks brown and broken, its leaves like disused rags slumped on the bank. As early as March its erect bright green shoots appear, curled ready to unwrap and to burst into rampant growth and height.

Behind me, the North American chestnut shrub (Blackeye), splendid in summer with its upright candles and leaves, and utterly insignificant in winter.

Opposite page
Left: Pen sketches of the pond
through the seasons
Bottom right: *Gunnera. Watercolour*

Right: Weed on the surface.
Ink & watercolour
Below left: Pond in Winter. *Watercolour*
Below right: **Round the Pond**.
Strong spring light. *Oil*, 30 × 30 cm

Summer

I sit in the tallest turkey oak's shade.
At full 50 feet, the lowest branches
Are ponderously pliant. Children swing,
Fanning the noon air, as heat blanches
The sky – but not the blue of damselflies.
One lights on my book: stilled wing,
Throbbing tail, twitching bulbous eyes,
Scanning the page for true likenesses made.

Ah, sad poems, said Lorca, strewn outdoors
Might bring poor insects to desolation!
Take care of all, especially the least,
As you join – with open invitation –
July's grasshoppers at their nuptial feast,
The wildflower meadow's shrill, rasping amours.

Adrian Blamires

Wavelengths. The trimmed
hedges behind the red
borders. *Oil*, 60 × 60 cm

Opposite page
The Path through the Grass.
Under the cherries in summer.
Pastel, 32 × 32 cm

Below left: Prairie. *Watercolour*
Below right: **Tea for Two**. At an
Open Sunday. *Pastel, 32 × 32 cm*

July

The Garden looking lush and almost overgrown, giving a slight suggestion of decadence after nearly two months of rainfall. Flowers normally finished, yet still vigorous in height and bloom. Formal borders reaching over eight feet tall!

The first of my drawing workshops in the Harris Garden mercifully missed the showers, allowing students to access it after the morning tuition session. As this was on one of the monthly Open Days it meant the opening up of the 'secret' Walled Garden ... as well as tea and cakes!

At the edge of the Formal Garden, I leave behind the dark hedges, proceeding past the Prairie Garden of golden *Rudbeckia* and to the wildness beyond.

The meadow filled with flowers, grasses and the Cherry Bowl, white in spring, red in autumn, currently green and wrapped in pink.

Flowering highlights:
· Agapanthus, Gravel Border
· Turtlehead (*Chelone*)
· Eucryphia
· Fuchsia
· Hydrangeas
· Lilies
· Penstemon
· Persicaria
· False dragon head (*Physostegia*)
· Gravel Border
· Miller Border
· Mixed Border
· Red Border

August

My second workshop and many students chose to paint in the Walled Garden, the hoods and umbrellas that they had brought as a precaution for the July day now replaced with sun hats.

The box hedges add a geometric pattern to this enclosed space with the shaped bay trees offering shade. The brick walls indicate that there were once grand south-facing greenhouses, alas now gone. Dill and daisies, sweet peas and a bed of melons, or are they pumpkins? Or gourds? A central pond and rows of vegetables ... Now here I really could pitch my tent!

The borders crammed with flowers in full high summer, with the Red Border hot and humming. The Gravel Garden is enjoying the heat of mid-August, so too the Jungle Garden, which seems almost to have become tropical. Anti-malaria tablets were even joked about by the volunteers!

Far left: In the Jungle Garden. *Watercolour*
Left: In the borders. *Watercolour*

Opposite page
Left: Tutored day, students sketching. *Pen & wash*
Above right: **In the Walled Garden**. A sketching and painting workshop day. *Pastel, 32 × 32 cm*
Below right: **Midsummer**. *Pastel, 23 × 23 cm*

Opposite page
Eucalyptus. *Pastel*, 18 × 23 cm

Left: Autumn. *Watercolour*
Right: **The Dead-Hedge**. Towards the fruit trees in early autumn.
Oil, 30 × 30 cm

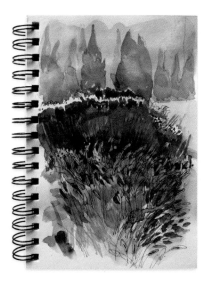

September

Final Open Day of the year in September and the Garden is looking great, the volunteers having worked really hard. Autumn on the way.

The conifers, evergreen, are unchanged. The large eucalyptus by the Gravel Garden with its distinctive smell, continuously sloughing off dead curls of bark, which hang and whisper like Chinese chimes as I sketch.

A crescent-shaped path defines a secluded small garden known as the Autumn Border. It has been reclaimed and replanted, the brambles weeded away from the banks, the overhanging trees trimmed back to let in more light, and their branches shredded to provide woodchip for the paths. The beautiful rich colours are at their best this month, pink to coppery-red sedums, deep rose-purple anemones, pink cyclamen and purple-leafed berberis.

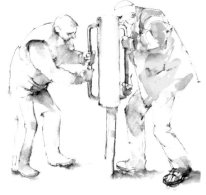

Opposite page
Left: Planting the magnolia.
Pen & wash
New fence post. *Pen & wash*
Monica and Dave mulching the
main border. *Pen & wash*
Right: **Forward Looking**. November
sun breaking through the morning
mist. *Pastel*, 23 × 30 cm

Below: Winter tea break. *Watercolour*
Giles planting in the Autumn Border.
Pen & wash
Right: Gravel Garden. *Watercolour*

People

I felt from the outset that the people who work here and love this Garden – Friends and volunteers – needed to be featured in my study as they do so much. I have been amazed at what an enormous impact a team of a dozen or so volunteers can have in a morning as far as clearing, weeding and planting goes. Not to mention organising Open Days and preparing the teas and the cakes and the plant sales.

Autumn

We gather late September light in sheaves,
The year's last true warmth, and crop
The crab apple orchard's ornamental
Harvest of names: Golden Hornet, Liset,
John Downie, Profusion, Red Sentinel.
The last proves a portent, seems to elicit
A russet watchfulness through yellowing leaves,
A line of stink that brings us to this stop:

How stilled we are, meeting the fox,
My redhead wife and son, and I; how hushed
The drone of traffic from Wilderness Road;
And how pointed the brushoff (end of episode)
As, turning tail, he steps, deft, unrushed,
Into the Eco-Zone, over the equinox.

Adrian Blamires

Dried Heads.
Pastel, 23 × 23 cm

October

Walking towards the Cherry Bowl, which looked so magnificent in blossom in the spring and again with pink summer grasses. Now it suddenly claims another award as the leaves have turned to glowing red and the grasses to white.

And I'm thinking back to what was a pure space, earlier in the year, the White Garden. Now the stage-set has changed – a dramatic transformation into the brilliant orange of the beech hedges.

Round by the Conservation Zone hedge, the space has been cleared, and subsequently planted with hazel trees. The meadow never disappoints, even with bleached grasses and dried seed-heads.

Below left: Autumn. *Ink & watercolour*
Below right: **The Mist Beyond**.
Beech hedges in autumn sun.
Oil, 30 × 30 cm

Opposite page
Conifers. *Pastel*, 18 × 23 cm

Below left: The cut meadow.
Wash & watercolour
Below right: **To Mow the Meadow**.
One man and his machine.
Oil, 30 × 30 cm

Opposite page
Fronds. The Miller Border welcoming
winter. *Pastel, 23 × 23 cm*

November

An alarming sight: the mowing of the meadow, the flowers and all those wonderful grasses suddenly gone, like a young child's curls being cropped. The foliage diminished and the views expanded. But the low autumn sun is shining through the dust of the cuttings, as the mower makes its way up and down leaving behind that banded pattern I like so much.

The bananas protected once more, like the other tender plants which have been moved under cover. Plants trimmed down in most borders, but the Miller Border plants left standing tall, dark and handsome, and consequently often looking mysterious. But beautiful, whether sunlit or rigid with frost. Fungi appearing overnight in the far meadow. Clearing, mulching and planting for next spring.

Flowering highlights:
- Strawberry tree, bark (*Arbutus x andrachnoides*)
- St Patrick's cabbage (*Bergenia* 'Wintermärchen')
- Silver birch (*Betula*)
- Dogwoods (*Cornus*)
- Crab apple, fruits (*Malus sylvestris*)
- Seed heads in the Miller Border
- Hollies (*Ilex*)
- Large collection of conifers around the Garden
- Gravel Garden
- Winter Garden

Below left: Volunteers in the potting shed. *Pen & wash*
Below right: **Icing**. Ice crystals on the fruit trees. *Pastel, 32 × 32 cm*

Opposite page
New Year's Eve. *Pastel, 23 × 23 cm*

December

Days in December always are short and dark and, this year, very wet. I found it an unexpected challenge to paint and record such days. Painters thrive on light and how it plays on the landscape – elusive and exciting. Now, there are no shadows and almost no colour.

On such inclement days the volunteers are to be found in what is called 'the potting shed', but is actually a large building with a central bench for the job in hand.

Reflecting on this Garden, flanked as it is by the wooded area of the wilderness to my left (still part of the University grounds), I can understand the campus as a whole being awarded (two years running) Green Flag status, national recognition of its importance to the community.

And I pay my tribute to someone I never knew, to Antony Miller who died in 1996, who made a substantial bequest to this Garden to secure its future.

New Year's Eve was an intensely dark day. New Year's Day: bright and sunny. And so another cycle is born.

History of the Garden

Pete's shed. *Watercolour*

The Harris Garden sits in the southern corner of Whiteknights Park, part of the manor of Erleigh (or Earley), which was owned by generations of the De Erleigh family until 1365. John de Erleigh IV was the 'White Knight' who gave his name to the park. After several changes in ownership and occupancy, Whiteknights was bought in 1798 by George Spencer, Marquis of Blandford, who spent more money than he possessed on his library, his gardens and on entertaining. In 1819 Spencer, by now Duke of Marlborough, was declared bankrupt. The Duke escaped to Blenheim, the Oxfordshire seat of the Marlboroughs, but Whiteknights went through a long period of decline. Whiteknights House was demolished in 1840 and in 1867 the park was divided into six leaseholds, each with a more modest house, three of which (Erleigh Park, The Wilderness and Foxhill) were designed by the distinguished Victorian architect Alfred Waterhouse (the last for him to live in), who also made additions to the house called Whiteknights. In 1947 the University of Reading acquired all six leaseholds, reunited Whiteknights Park as an entity and began its expansion from the old site on London Road.

The Harris Garden has its origins in the University's botanic garden, which was laid out in 1972 when the Departments of Botany and Agricultural Botany moved from London Road to the new Plant Science Laboratories (now the Harborne Building). The Botanic Garden occupied what had once been the home paddock of The Wilderness, one of the six houses of the 1860s but demolished in the 1940s. The site was spacious but there was little money available to develop the Garden. Some plants came from the Department of Agricultural Botany's former garden at Shinfield and many more were raised from seed by Ronnie Rutherford, the garden's curator, and planted out into the meadow, a woodland area on the Pepper Lane boundary and around a newly made pond. The

Towards the pond. *Watercolour*

main evidence of intensive gardening lay in three beds near the entrance of the garden devoted to medicinal plants, variegated plants and pelargoniums.

In 1987 the Department of Horticulture and Landscape moved to Whiteknights from its former home at Shinfield. In 1988, with the arrival of the head gardener Alan Hayes and four other staff from Shinfield, work began to extend and enhance the Botanic Garden to meet the wider teaching and research requirements of the enlarged School of Plant Sciences. In recognition of its new, wider role, the Botanic Garden was renamed the Harris Garden. This not only commemorates the late Professor Tom Harris, a distinguished Reading palaeobotanist and renowned gardener, but also acknowledges the long contribution made by Miss Elspeth Harris in developing the horticultural garden at Shinfield Grange, the design of which influenced the layout of the new Harris Garden. The boundary of the Garden was extended to include the 1860 walled garden belonging to The Wilderness.

The early years of the Harris Garden were what the Chinese would term 'interesting'. Many trees were lost in the storms of 1987 and 1990, including a lime which had been the tallest tree in the Garden. The Garden, like the campus as a whole, was plagued by rabbits. The garden staff ringed the whole Garden with rabbit-proof netting, but were not allowed to shoot the rabbits already living in the Garden. However, a combination of trapping and ferreting gradually reduced the rabbit population so that planting could begin in earnest. A basic irrigation system of pipes and standpipes was installed but it took months of negotiation to persuade Thames Water that the University should not be required to pay an additional sewerage charge as there would be no waste emanating from the water used for irrigation.

Left: Cherry Bowl blossom.
Pen & wash
Right: **Cherry Orchard**.
Pastel, 32 × 32 cm

Opposite page
Above: First flowering of the
species tulips. *Watercolour*
Below: Full summer. *Watercolour*

Eventually thoughts turned to implementing the 1987 design by Richard Bisgrove, lecturer in Landscape Management. Although there were many interesting plants throughout the Garden, the overall impression of the 12 acre (5 hectare) Garden was of an open expanse of rough grass with a few large trees, including the impressive turkey oaks (*Quercus cerris*) near the entrance, planted in 1830 and 1860. There was no evidence of Alexander Pope's famous advice in his 1731 *Epistle* that 'He gains all points, who pleadingly confounds, / Surprises, varies, and conceals the bounds.'

In the 1980s there had been much research by the Forestry Commission on tree establishment, so a decision was made that the Garden would incorporate some of the results of this research in demonstration plots. 1,440 trees of ten native species were planted by the Horticulture students with some trees in grass, some in bare ground, some mulched, some in tree tubes and so on. For the first few years each cohort of new students measured the trees and drew their conclusions. Surprisingly quickly the 'New Wood' sprang up, a long chain of young trees through the middle of the long axis of the Garden, creating around it a necklace of open space which could then be developed as a series of garden ideas.

The paperbark maple (*Acer griseum*), with its peeling orange bark, just inside the entrance to the Garden, was one of the first new trees, given by that year's Horticulture finalists.

Soon after the designation of the Harris Garden a group of Friends was formed at the instigation of Dr Stephen Jury, a research fellow in Botany, who chaired the group until his retirement in 2012. The Friends have given much support in the development of the Garden. 'The Orchard' of crab apples near the entrance to the Garden, underplanted with bulbs, cowslips and ox-eye daisies, was paid for by them as was a new pond liner in 1995 and materials for the Stream Garden created in 2000, amongst other gifts. A Winter Garden at the entrance, an Autumn Bank half way along the north-west boundary and a Cherry Bowl of Japanese flowering cherries towards the northern end of the Garden near the Walled Garden, were early components of the chain of features around the perimeter of the Garden. In the open centre of the Garden a cluster of hedged compartments accommodate or accommodated a little formal garden, a rose garden, borders of annuals and other colourful plantings.

From the stream. *Mixed media*

In 2010 the School of Biological Sciences relinquished responsibility for the Harris Garden. Its development and maintenance were handed over to the University's Grounds team headed by Giles Reynolds. Rather than this resulting in a retrograde simplification of the Garden with acres of gang-mown grass, as many had feared, the Harris Garden took on a new lease of life. Many thousands of bulbs have been planted; large areas of flowering meadow have been sown; hedges have been reshaped and many of the early features of the Garden have been replaced, refreshed or regenerated.

Gardens are ephemeral works of art. The original concept for the Harris Garden was to create a necklace of small gardens within a larger framework, a necklace which could be revisited periodically and reinvigorated. This concept was instigated in 1987 and the policy of refreshment and revision is being actively pursued, so the Garden looks set fair to flourish as an important and much loved retreat in a corner of the Whiteknights campus.

Richard Bisgrove
School of Biological Sciences,
University of Reading

Opposite page
Meteoric. In the White Garden.
Pastel, 32 × 32 cm

Two Rivers Press has been publishing in and about Reading since 1994. Founded by the artist Peter Hay (1951–2003), the press continues to delight readers, local and further afield, with its varied list of individually designed, thought-provoking books.

The Harris Garden is on the Whiteknights campus of the University of Reading, and is an important amenity open to all. The Friends of the Harris Garden is an organisation which was formed in 1987 to support the development of the Garden, in partnership with the University.

The role of the Friends is to promote activities in, and connected with, the Harris Garden, and to further the development of its amenities and educational services. The Friends have funded various significant features within the Garden such as the stream and new bulb planting. The appointment of an Artist in Residence for 2012 was an exciting opportunity, culminating in supporting an exhibition and this book.

friends of the
HARRIS
GARDEN